DIASPORIC
VIETNAMESE
ARTISTS
NETWORK

DVAN FOUNDERS

ISABELLE THUY PELAUD
AND
VIET THANH NGUYEN

Also in the series:

Constellations of Eve, by Abbigail Nguyen Rosewood

Hà Nội at Midnight: Stories, by Bảo Ninh; translated and edited by
Quan Manh Ha and Cab Tran

Nothing Follows, by Lan P. Duong

*Watermark: Vietnamese American Poetry & Prose, 25th Anniversary
Edition*, edited by Barbara Tran, Monique Truong, and Khoi Luu

DROWNING DRAGON SLIPS BY BURNING PLAINS

POEMS

KHẢI ĐƠN

TEXAS TECH UNIVERSITY PRESS

This book is typeset in EB Garamond. The paper used in this book meets the minimum requirements of ANSI/NISO Z39.48-1992 (R1997). ⊚

Designed by Hannah Gaskamp
Cover designed by Hannah Gaskamp
Interior artwork by Hung Viet Nguyen

Library of Congress Cataloging-in-Publication Data

Names: Khải Đơn, 1987– author. Title: Drowning Dragon Slips by Burning Plains: Poems / Khải Đơn. Description: Lubbock, Texas: Texas Tech University Press, 2023. | Series: DVAN | Summary: "Through poems and images, a local reveals the true history of the Mekong Delta."—Provided by publisher. Identifiers: LCCN 2023012936 | ISBN 978-1-68283-193-9 (cloth) Subjects: LCGFT: Poetry. Classification: LCC PR9560.9.K43 D76 2023 | DDC 821/.92—dc23/ eng/20230714 LC record available at https://lccn.loc.gov/2023012936

Printed in the United States of America
23 24 25 26 27 28 29 30 31 / 9 8 7 6 5 4 3 2 1

Texas Tech University Press
Box 41037
Lubbock, Texas 79409-1037 USA
800.832.4042
ttup@ttu.edu
www.ttupress.org

To Chalu, my philosopher of loving life

CONTENTS

CONTENTS

ACKNOWLEDGMENTS

My deepest gratitude to every person from the Mekong Delta who fed me sour soup and bitter rice, who whispered their life stories into my years of becoming, who has loved the rivers sincerely and watched them erode in great sorrow.

This book is made possible with the professional guidance and kindness of poet and Professor J. Michael Martinez, Professor Alan Soldofsky, and Dr. Linda Mitchell. My dear writing fellows Addie Mahmassani and Felipe de la Rosa have been patiently guiding me through the joy and whirpool of writing in a foreign language.

I am grateful to artist Nguyen Viet Hung for all the artwork he created with incredible creative energy featured in this book.

Thank you Crossing Borders Grants from Berlin for believing in my work since its very early stages and giving me the luxury of time to work on the first idea for a year. The US Department of State's Fulbright Foreign Student Program has given me the necessary scholar training at San José State University to craft the lyrics for every poem. The Diasporic Vietnamese Artists Network (DVAN) and *diaCritics* tendered early encouragement to approach writing beyond my mother tongue.

PROLOGUE

I invite you to venture into my world: The Mekong Delta—The land of abundance, The infinite horizon of rice, hiding a violent and faceless past.

One day, a piece of an island eroded into the Mekong River. I was standing by an old woman witnessing her land shredding itself away. Layers of earth flesh were exposed: brownish clay, red fertile soil, bright yellow sand, light gray gravel. The Mekong Delta is sinking into the sea because of climate change and greedy development.

In the soil, the past forms billowing smoke rising from deaf eardrums. The past erodes, sandbanks carving, children chasing traveling ghosts. My neighbors are generous. They are kind to murderers who overturned their ancestors' altars. They forgive powerful hands slaughtering their swamps and choking river paths, from French colonization through the American War to the communists' relentless consumption.

I search my path of writing, a blind child wandering in mazes of forgetfulness. The reality is too painful to recollect. Many wars passed, genocides taking place. Those hurt by bloodshed avoid talking about it; those benefiting from conflicts brag without hesitation. We lie to each other to live on without being tortured by our conscience. History unpeels itself like layers of soil, painstakingly, with cruel kindness. I eat falsehoods and digest forgetfulness.

Like my eroding land in the Mekong Delta, deep layers of truth and sincerity crouch beneath a terrifying surface. At the same time, I consciously know that I would not witness the vibrancy of truth without the delta's being consumed by the sea and suffocating under the concrete greed of the new dawn.

I run into the arms of my river.

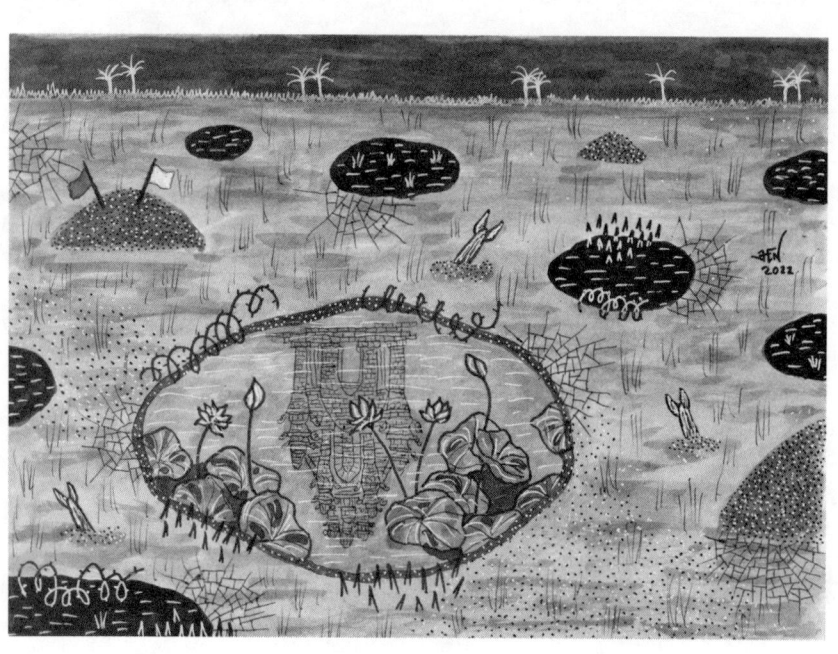

DROWNING
DRAGON
SLIPS BY
BURNING
PLAINS

ONE DAY AFTER THE PEACEFUL TIME

Flying bombs turn mangoes in my grandma's garden; juicy flesh I
bite in red summers.

Craters hold fermented pomelo; lime pink water glints the
sour sunsets.

Lotuses bloom over massacres; pollinating the river, remains' eyes
stare at ripened seedpods.

Sweet rice grows on potters' fields, feeding young girls
tickling breezes.

Buddha Master's body gathers at sea, bursting into swarms of
illuminating *linh* fish.

The ghost theatre plays a loving act: Departed soldiers kiss rotten
wives in tidal swamps.

At the end of this,

I row a leafy boat to the razed jungle, making eye contact with the
mythical crocodile.

Mangroves tangle and grow out of my shins.

DURIAN FLESH

Threads of durian scent tangle my hair
a void fills in where it used to be the fruit garden I slept
my years of infancy. I was not drawn
to the hallucination of fluorescent
light; suicidal moths, but here
I am, getting lost in a square
box sweatshop, wishing
to grow mayfly wings, seeking high
moments beaming flash into my chest –
That braveness [or] desperation carves meaning
out of the starving water; I carve myself
off the groves of hungered soil, dragging
to the surface of wealthiness, almost non-
- existent in my father's durian garden
He dug and planted seedlings until we
had the first durian young soft skin
we sunk our teeth in the sweetest bite
of Mekong heaven. O, Heaven
dried up and peeled its skin on the scorched
field blistering my palms. Now I stand
under the excruciating lights; flapping
my exhausted moth wings
Memories of
home flutters
flutt-flut-er- er
-er -e

A DREAM OF RETURNING

You wander through the hill as the clouds are threading the river arms. You braid the foaming layers like you used to braid your little sister's cloudy hair. Now you stand in the middle of the braided hill. The wind brushes the foam-lipped eddies, where you used to swim and flap water in her giggles. The light is so bright, and you lose your way uphill. You lost your way to her. Again. You stand among exquisite flying threads, you see a catfish leap through thickets toward you. But when he goes up close, you realize he is not a fish but your sister who used to cry with you in the schoolyard when your mom forgot to pick both of you up. It was when you were six and your sister was four and mom showed up with purple bruises on her left eye while you were braiding your sister's hair. The bruise was as deep as as the river's soul, her eyes reddened as the sun floating in. After the summer, your sister never returned to school. You couldn't remember where she went since she faded away too quick. She was playing with dirt in the front garden. She didn't turn back to look at you. Your mind braided itself to the hill but it does not braid her smile back to you. She walks among the silky hills and her shadow casts on your feet. You scream at her: "Why do you never return?" But it is late. You are both late for class. The school gate shuts its mouth, swallows your mother's sun eyes. All the lessons crumble into dirt and you can't remember if either of you exist.

ON BECOMING

The flood peeks at our mother's door. Mother lifts her arms, reaching her tentacles to the river edge. The mud house wails a flood's song. Rice pots clank their mouth in the pace of

water

D
R
I
P

S. Our forest bounces the tree limbs on spreading ripples. The flood pumps itself into my vein, the dikes of my heart. We build concrete dikes for centuries because we fear the flood because we cannot stand its enormous manifestation of our quiet and ignored existence because the flood wipes out all our wrongdoings to each other because we choke the flood with the rotten remains of our ancestors. The flood carries their hair and eyes through rice fields through smoke veils on harvest twilight through folk songs through the frogs jumping off the ocean seeking its furthest horizon, quivering in our tiny cells growing fetus in our mothers' bellies, sucking the flood the gray milk stream sprouting us seedling us floating us devouring us. The giant catfish watches us like their pet kittens. Our river sways with us in the dancing duckweeds. We swim. Drowned. Swim [again]. And we start walking in two infant feet.

BURNING RICE

Dad told me he had to leave home
since the earth turned its back on us,
and hunger hollowed my flooded eyes

The soil broke into dust
wilted leaves curved a bending sky
roots metallic and murky
sour famine rose in my throat

My grandpa's iris—opaline milk
tapped into the flattened sun
Salty streams crawled up to green
pigments, dying grains pale brown.

Then the rice field knelt exhausted
Dad burnt the last acre
I peeled out his arms
The muted breeze brushed us
                    off each other

He strayed among the fish farms
gutting and chopping heads
thousand bloody times
whatever he would   kill
                    to feed me

I nibbled the scorched grains
grandpa gleaned through meager harvest

Why the rice field abandoned us
I croaked with
frogs and   ------ the aloneness--------
            cast------ me
                        -----into the---
                                ---swamp----

DRUNKEN PAST

I float on the rice wine
      harvested by my mother's rough hands
      fluffy up in Mekong water --- grayish alluvium
      fermented on my sweaty skin --- alcohol evaporated
      my father tending the flickering flames -- burning sorrow

Hot liquid blooms my torso
      blackouts angered memories
      naked tongue papillae burns
      the monstrous truth in my chest

We have drunk enough to forget a century
      Winning soldiers marinated bitterness
      swing their legs towards loved ones
      Losing soldiers drank the ocean
      on the festered sea of pirates

My father has drunk enough to stop seeing
      me --- sitting at his eye corners, begging for a head
      pat, reminding I am still his child
      germinating from his lullabies

I have drunk enough to be poisoned
      hot liquor evaporates the men's smirks
      reaping me apart --- a feast
      naked in fangs of honorable predators

We have drunk enough to wash off
        our last crumbs of tenderness,
        last shard of dignity,
        scattered memories of every beloveds
                choked in our hands.

DEAR MY BELOVEDS,

I am not a fleshy *longan* you squeezed
                    in a summer of yellow fever
I am not a half-naked singer in a karaoke parlor
                  wailing my grandfather's song for
                        your entertainment
I am not a blinded masseuse leading to a happy-
                            -ending you are ghosted of
I am not an illiterate daughter, hands calloused in endless
                        toilet cleaning jobs
I am not the nail worker inhaling dust until lungs
                        scarred for her family's wealth
I am not an exported bride, strangled in
                        my foreign husband's bedroom
I am not an exhausted maid, milked to starve
                      for others' children and thrown
                      out on the street - childless
I am not the mother in fairy tales, squeezing her
                          drops of breath for husband's
                          children until whacked
I am not a garbage grandma wandering
                      into forever chemical extracting
                      cash for her grandchildren
My face
        fractured by my loved ones' greed.

FABLE OF ME-FOREST

My time stagnates in Mother's iris

The day we move to the forest, the Bear
groans on the glassy lake
Mushroom knobs brush my ankles
soft as a little squirrel's fur

Mother says: The Bear surmises us home
Although I don't know who the Bear is, I tiptoe
through the stripes of a quiet Python
hugging our house's pillar, meeting
the Bear's furrowed brows
Father says: when you drowse,
the Python slithers in
turning fairy tales into fanged fairies

Summer passes. The rainy season blooms
medang in my palms, potent yellow
petals tremble in the Bear's ears:
Mining men sashay with giant Caterpillars
loom on the leafage beds
The lake is rimmed in rusted foam
I drink a handful of metallic water

Finally, the Python sheds its skin
by our terrace, brown scales melt
The Bear roars every road collapse
It is our turn, Father says, say you love Forest, we leave
Why don't we carry the Forest, I ask Mother

The Forest sprouts in your lungs
open your throat, do you see the growth rings

In Mother's eyes, the lake rises
the Caterpillars' heads gasp bubbles
The dancing Bear chews their
newly grown wings. The Python
squeezes metal excavator's teeth
Father drools silk cocooning me
I wriggle in the walled-womb-me

DAUGHTER OF MANY WARS

Don't ask if I understand wars
I was a fetus from that bloodbath
A seedling grew from aftermaths
endless jungle raids to town assaults

I sucked my mother's nipples
bruised and delivering me from strikes
stirred her womb – a dirt tunnel
collapsed on her fluid break

My young mouth gaped for rice water
Dripping from leftovers of brotherhood
slaughters: my father fought his brother
when his brothers stabbed cousins when
his brother-in-law rotted in an island
prison as our grandmother counted
her sons' hands waving from
nameless dirt graves

My milk teeth grew from starving
farmers on blossoming rice flowers
My hair grew in reddened rivers
My skin the burning borders woven
the impunity of massacres

The coconut worm rolled in the fire
whistled the songs of the blind
bullets anonymously puncturing
holes on my mother's shinbone

I ran after fading kites in the sunset
dipped in the mourning songs of un-headed
soldiers heading homes - bomb craters
hollowed out demented war scraps

On the news, people crave for anger
tanks grind on mud paths, battleships landing
Our impulsive curiosity bleeds into mundane jokes
We gently entertain other's wars amid peace.

GRIEVOUS TREE

When your life is robbed from you
Your village: The Parrot's Beak on a strayed map
Your body: the toy of hammers
sickles, and helicopters
Your branches: threads of air
swerving into mountain caves
pungent is the fate of innocence.

Your bark drips fresh infants calling
moms whose breasts burst milk in the dust
your carved holes grab quiet heads
You: the collector of red grass.

We: skulls smirking from crystal shrines
Our eyes holes behind aluminum bars
ivory-white bones - songs of murders
crossing The Plain of Reeds
bare feet crushed our bare eyes

The Parrot's Beak starves in the
temple hiding our raw lips
No one wrote down our names
We lived unknown, died unknown
remains stuck in the strayed existence

You're standing on the crossroad
a perpetrator requiem

Do you remember our names?
our shreds dissolve
into soil fertility

Please remember
        Remem --- re---- ber
                    ---er----

The Grievous Tree of Ba Chúc: *A banyan tree witnessed the 12-day massacre in Ba Chúc village. No victims were helped; the village was left on its own in the killing spree of the Khmer Rouge.*

GLASSY LOTUS

I can't see her
the half-naked body crosses
another two motionless men
on the chess board
of three thousand pawns
sacrificed by borders

We didn't see enemies
just shadows in *kroma*
moving by
our smiling Buddha

Did Buddha grow fangs
or were there fangs in our stomach
one day we cannibalized?

I sway in the lotus shrine
counting finger bones
although there left no finger

ribcage piles sing songs
shinbones bounce
hunching the lotus necks

The dusk marigold blooms
on bare skulls, bare teeth
smile at my face

Behind encased reverence I hear
everyone cries although they
are crystallized white named
by numbers preserved
on glass shelves

They scream so quietly

On April 18, 1978, the Khmer Rouge began a massacre that ended in the killing of 3,157 people in Ba Chúc village. Victims' skulls and bones encased in glass boxes are exhibited in their bare afterlife existence in a lotus shrine. They never rest, even in peace.

Guillemot, François. "Autopsy of a Massacre on a Political Purge in the Early Days of the Indochina War (Nam Bo 1947)," *European Journal of East Asian Studies* 9, no. 2 (2010): 250.

O RIVER, our yellow skin red blood
    lying in restless stirs, ebb tides
          lies swarmed
          our children's
          deafened ears
      since when
          we only sing glossy
          cải lương
            furnish ourselves
            unto sorrow?
O River, we forget our kin
        Their faces queue
          to the stream of
            no return

O River, close your eyes
          Don't let us see our bloody
          hands.

DEAR ĐỨC THẦY,

Your Enlightenment hides under the storks'
flapping wings.

     Dismembered.

       Dissolving.

Now we called you the Water Mountain.

OLD MAN'S TALE IN NÚI CẤM

Forbidden Mountains cover their eyes
I walk in the twilight, an old man sings
lyrics scrub on floating fields:

I watched my father disappear
into the jaws of the black palm trees
I ran into his shadow, dispersing
into red petals of the phoenix
flowers immolated and dyed
the bleeding sky I fell into.

The black palm trees lift their
guns drilling holes into my father's
ankles a burning praying paper in Holy
Mother of the Realm's hand wounded
by the Siam's elephant's trunk twisting
liars' necks into piling rocks.

The rocks I am stepping on - invaders' traces
falling by the protector goddess's feet:

I saw my father's back
until bits of him were crushed
The future passed me in a blink
I still search for him in every rice grain

Each morning the sun blooms dripping
open injuries to black palm tree
gardens hanging bodies on their stained pyre.
My sun dimmed with his faded bà ba.

And I look at where the goddess's eyes closed---
a blank universe: *Bà Chúa Xứ* lost her faith
The black palm trees have grown
tentacles into her veins.

FABLE OF THE ERASED

Hòa Hảo religion was founded by a young man who named himself an incarnation
of Buddha Master of Western Peace in 1930s Vietnam. Thousands of its followers
were purged by the American-backed government and then the Communist regime.
Hòa Hảo Village permanently changed its name to Phú Tân [rich and new], erased
from modern times.

An abandoned market   a town of dark   disguises a peaceful village
                    a chorus of voided souls
                    never made their names over ripping tides.

An old man munches a rice leaf   slitting his
        tongue   bleeds one-by-one
                    into tiny human bodies   churning in
                                  churning out
                                    his lips
He arranges each one on a melaleuca table
                    Tiny people wriggle and lay quiet; prayers
                      quavered
He keeps pulling out more, thousands.   None have eyes or mouths
                    Searching for each other blindly.
                           On that table of fate
                    quietness blasted
Then he pulls each hair and more little people climb down to the
crowds, his head traces
                    the mark of a skull
                    hollowed
He holds my palms, slowly grinding bodies into gray
                    mixtures of abandoned:
                    memories

The crowd of tiny people cry. Their throats split   into a river wound
                        exposed to the hungry
                        water
                        he traces
                        the clogged lines on my palm, murmurs:
                That is how we lost everyone we loved.

                        I only see
                        river, I said.

INCARNATION

Tánh ngay thẳng ta không dời đổi,
Dầu tan xương nát thịt chẳng màng.
[Lines 129–30, Giác Mê Tâm Kệ
- Awakening, Huỳnh Phú Sổ]

My blind grandfather sipped a prayer
The Terror's tentacles gripped
the altar. Sutras billowed.
The army in *bà ba* ghosted behind, shredded
bodies dyeing the river in black.

Prayers foamed at grandpa's mouth
Suffocating him in sponges of upheavals

Twenty-year-old reincarnated Buddha
Master chanted by my dying grandfather's side -
A swarm of flies nibbled his eye sockets
Swarms of white cranes witnessed
Buddha's feet sinking in the mud field

At night Buddha Master was   stabbed
his heaving chest licked the metallic iron knife.
His thighs were chewed by the river;
assembled a prophecy. Villagers stomped
on puddles of blood.

Buddha's head was
                hung by the village gate.

The army cut open the sutras. Slew.
Piled up. Cawing ravens mocked
the path to total peace. Their gaping beaks caught
tangled strands of prayers. Buddha's bones   sang
                                                clanking

Decades after, I crossed by
Him on an altar photo at my grandma's home - reincarnated
and killed. Repeatedly. His watery eyes stared.
His frail palms draped the river. Bedrock lay
shinbones backed vocals   echoed

The army cleans up massacres offering
conciliation. Grandma prays
like a maniac: *He is secretly* ------
----- *alive*. The tocsin is bruised,
crunching my fingers. We perform
                              the forgiveness

IRONY OF ABUNDANCE

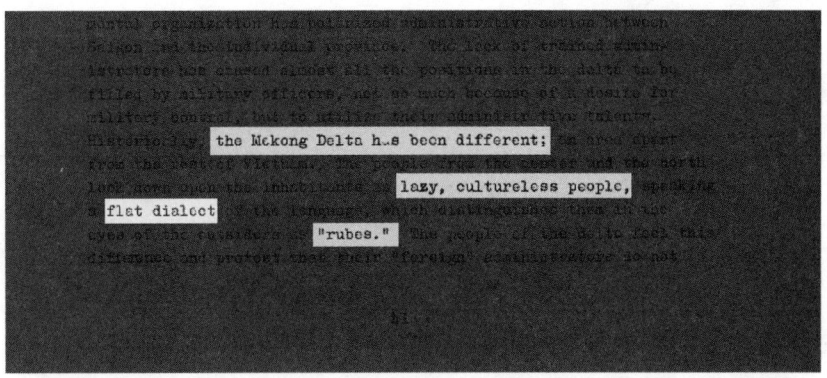

...mental organization has paralyzed administrative action between Saigon and the individual provinces. The lack of trained administrators has caused almost all the positions in the delta to be filled by military officers, not so much because of a desire for military control, but to utilize their administrative talents. Historically, the Mekong Delta has been different; an area apart from the rest of Vietnam. Its people from the center and the north look down upon the inhabitants as lazy, cultureless people, speaking a flat dialect. The farmer, as such, distinguishes them in the eyes of the outsiders as "rubes." The people of the delta feel this difference and protest that their "foreign" administrators do not...

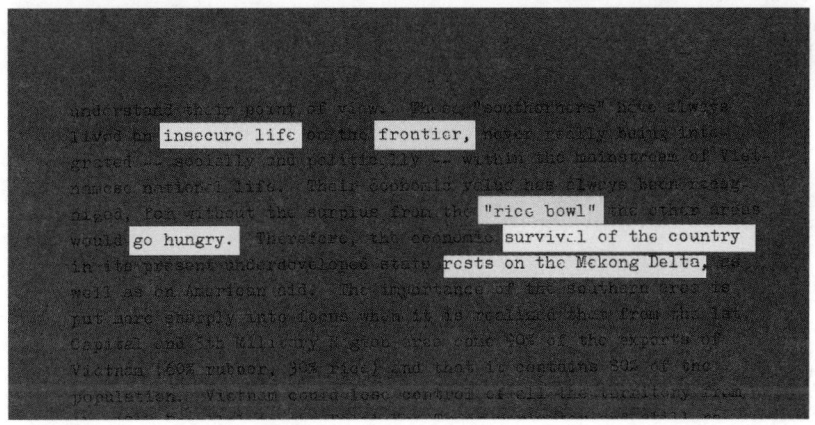

...understand their point of view. These "southerners" have always lived an insecure life on the frontier, never really being integrated — socially and politically — within the mainstream of Vietnamese national life. Their economic value has always been recognized, for without the surplus from the "rice bowl" the other areas would go hungry. Therefore, the economic survival of the country in its present underdeveloped state rests on the Mekong Delta, as well as on American aid. The importance of the Southern area is put more sharply into focus when it is realized that from the 1st Capital and 5th Military Regions come 50% of the exports of Vietnam (60% rubber, 80% rice) and that it contains 80% of the population. Vietnam considers control of all the territory such...

DISPOSITION FORM	SECURITY CLASSIFICATION *(if any)*
	SECRET

FILE NO. MAGPL	SUBJECT Revised Draft Study, Internal Security Problem, SVN (U)		
TO CHMAAG	FROM Actg Ch, Plans Div, Exec Gp	DATE 9 Jan 61	COMMENT NO. 1

TWO   FATES

We get starved in a   *rice bowl*
Our illiterate Buddha is   *cultureless*
Our bodies stood
        naked
                for the   *survival of the country*
        Our ancestors' cells   *prosperity sediment*
        Our daughters' cheeks   *juicy mangoes*

                grow   *from dismembered*
                                         faith

STOP TALKING ABOUT US AS IF YOU KNEW

Written for the Vietnam Vets I met mentioned
names of battlefields as sweet memories

Remember *Watchmen*? - When The Comedian shot
    a woman in creamy *bà ba*, her forehead spilled
    liquid on her swollen belly
    Even the charming hems cannot save her
    from your massacre in Hollywood

Stop showing off where you fought in the '60s
    how many medals you got
    you returned to Quảng Trị
    or crawled into Củ Chi Tunnel
    eating cassava sweet like sesame
                    or mortars

Stop bragging about Khe Sanh
    or your buddy saved your neck in Huế
    stop admiring the Vietcong and
    staring at shattered
    young boys lying by Tân Sơn Nhứt
    runways

Stop war-porning us
    masturbating your tiny ego
    in a swamp you drown every
    frog to bloated

Stop dreaming us in your pleasure dream
           splitting *áo dài* and slender arms
           you used to rape them in the sweaty
           monsoon of Saigon

Stop groping us in your hyper imagination
           you return home with no legs or penis
           we lost our Buddha
           our dignity, every fragment of it you
           burnt in your wet dream of America

Stop admiring our country so green
           fuck you it used to be green in the crocodile eyes
           before your B52 festivals napalm fireworks
           before the communists' greed to get rich, sniffing
           your green dollars

But does it really matter,
how green or how barren, our jungles
between our legs were spread countless
times to make up your oblivious dream
of saving us from ourselves

BRIDGING THE UNKNOWN

... the death toll from the collapse to around 60, officials said.
As many as 180 were injured, some of them suffering critical head
wounds, in Wednesday morning's collapse of a section of a Japa-
nese-funded bridge under construction in the southern Mekong Delta.
Some 250 workers were on site at the time.

CAN THO, Vietnam (Reuters) – September 26, 2007

CONCRETE RAIN

Nobody was punished for their wrongdoings.

Officials said rains may have softened the foundations
so the giant bridge rains on workers' flesh
mincing them to pieces, perpetuating the land of fertility,
organic matter — softened foundation
dissolving fathers and sons in the rain of wealth.

Contractors, regulators will draw a lesson to overcome
its consequences – officials whispered the curse
suffusing water until it weaves a
prophet, raining young men into lifeless
wooden altars.
The rain wipes
clean contractors' faces erased
regulators unto nameless.

"I visited many families. I share their pain.
These pains are extreme," says the then president

---

*All the italicized lines are quotes from this news article: https://www.reuters.com/
article/us-vietnam-bridge-collapse/more-bodies-recovered-from-vietnam-bridge-
collapse-idUSHAN25222720070927.

As though he felt how intestines gouged, rained
out of bellies by steel pillars, as though he begot
a child whose face was ground into a rain puddle,
as though the bridge rained itself on humans, as if
young men still had their mouths
— untorn — unwedged — ungagged

as if he were even

once

        honest
        to the lifeless faces.

Bridge to offer route to rich property projects

Can Tho makes up for lost time

Hau Giang is ready to prosper

The scene of the devastation shortly after the collapse and generated widespread global coverage. Photo: Mai

Piecing together Can Tho's bridge tragedy

Bridge to transform a region

The rivers of change

Province wants to be at the crossroads of local trade

UNDER THE VANISHED BRIDGE

The sun unveils dark
young men's laughter bounces
off the coffee shop's thatch.
Concrete arms strangle
the river goddess's neck.

Sweaty men gulp down coffee float
on condensed milk, their jokes bleed into the night.

An old man, eye tails cracking like a barren
field, drops his sickle, chewing ice cubes.

His song: *Disgraced fields are unforgiving.*
Black herons tear angers.
Squawk wails in the humid wind.

The workers cracked a laugh:
Old man, bland joke. Land does not betray.
Our grandmothers fed us the milk from dust.

A young man hands a billiards cue to
his twin brother, weaving time on the moon shape,
walks into the tunnel bamboo flute
Exits are unseen.

Cải lương smears in the radio, intertwining
herons' **squawk**.

The bridge folds its stomach

        Squeaked
           cascading
                scaffolds
             girders   flood
             wooden slabs   typhoon
                metal beams   rain
                     cement
                    swamp

The other twin sees his feet hardened
in concrete. He watches himself
die. Twice.

The old man thrashes his feet in a pool of metal
scraps. Wiggling. He swims away in a mud carp soul.

Workers vaporize in the dust storm
Squawk. Choking herons' throats.

Fluid steel runs through farmers' marrows
        constructing a bridge of not-hunger.

               Of not-smearing-mud
                    on ankles
               Of not-hopeful
               Squawk   -hopelessness.

Their faces sink under gravel
and now scrubbed clean on newspapers.

An oil lamp licks my eyelids open
The   truth at the thick humid noon
sings an ancient
    Squawk
        song:

       Startling fly through the sun, following rivers to a far land
       Loving, loving each other, sharing a rice grain in half –

           sharing a grand bridge in half

I dig my brain out of the head socket, searching
for the past munching my memory like the   **Squawk** dead
heron.

      We gather in a coffee shop
          since the time
   all of   **Squawk**   us were alive.

WRITING MY PAST INTO YOUR PRESENT OF WATCHING THE DISGRACED TRUTH

1. Chinese author Yiyun Li once described the effect in *before and after* advertisements for plastic surgeries or hair-loss treatments as "the definitiveness of that phrase, before and after, with nothing muddling the in-between" in her memoir *Dear Friend, from My Life I Write to You in Your Life* (Li, chap. 1). The essay poses a question of how we are transformed in constant responses from outer life and our inner selves, between stages of our private life and our public performance, from our past self to our present self, and if a future self is waiting for us somewhere beyond us.

2. I nurture the past mostly because it is more honest to me than the present, which cascades into arguments and clashes, hurting me with its wobble facades and distorted kaleidoscope shards.

3. On a September morning in 2007, a half-built Cần Thơ Bridge collapsed. I know where the bridge is; it is being built next to my grandmother's district, a five-minute bike ride. I took a bus there to observe because I was 20 years old, and the tender existence of a young adult drew me towards dramatic disasters.

4. On the bus trip, my mind ventured to the past. There was no bridge in my childhood. I sat on my mother's lap, eating coconut candy, fresh pineapple, and sweet banana-rice paper mixed with the diesel smell from over 20 trucks and buses queuing by the ferry and waiting across the river on a slow ferry. The river smells like fish sauce, rice cake, and banana. The river carried lives on its skin and in its veins.

5. Then there is the bridge: collapsing. For some reason, I am

not curious how it would look at the monstrous moment. The Mekong with a slow ferry waits, no bridge, and pineapples piling up inviting tropical scent. That vision melted in my chest, heaving up and down, drowsy, enough for me to close my eyes and not question what I was about to see in three hours.

6. I have a trust issue with the present. It transforms like snakes, sneaking between facts and assumptions, between desire and capability, between imagination and reality, between newspapers and erased papers. It sheds the old skin, shrugging off and slipping into the present, like new, no trace back to the old shell. I struggle between the entanglement of snakes, with other thready snaky bodies, my journalist colleagues and me to weave a "truth" out for the daily manifestation of life, slipping and deforming. We tangle each other up like wool balls of snake in the hand of a cat-god, playful and untrustworthy, betraying its every moment.

7. I was invited to dinner with a reader. This man, a doctor trained by renowned French institutes, famous in his field, opened the door for me at a restaurant. His elegance struck me with the luxurious life I had never tasted. "I want to celebrate your braveness. You dare to tell the truth. Our country needs young people like you." He mentioned an article series I wrote about the child sex abuse situation in the Mekong Delta, where the police sided with perpetrators. I quietly wonder which truth he meant.

8. Near the bridge collapse site, I slept in the hospital yard with victims' families, where doctors and nurses rushed out to call names to ask for approvals for emergency surgeries. My mind blended into the slimy dark. An old woman next to me genuflected deeply. She changed direction four times and finished with a low bend on the gravel ground. "I prayed the Buddha to bless my sons." She pointed at the hospital's bright lobby leading to the emergency hall. Her twin sons were pulled out

of the concrete mass that morning.

9. Three days after the bridge collapsed, 59 young male work-
    ers died. 180 others were seriously injured. The Ministry of
    Transportation announced that the bridge collapsed *maybe*
    because of the rain. I cocooned myself in the past, wrapping
    tight enough to not explode into the present.

10. I grew up in this part of the Mekong Delta; the rain didn't kill
    people.

11. I learn Taekwondo. The practice required me to pay attention
    to my belly. I kick thousands of times, aiming at the belly area.
    Soft spot. Immediate injury. No matter how strong the fighter
    is, not protecting the belly might come with great harm later
    into the long combat. Protecting the belly becomes a matter
    of winning or losing.
    If I let my guard down and the present kicks me in my belly, I
    lose.

12. In a communist country, the present is an adjusted version of
    the past, one of many, because the present of the tomorrow
    might be adjusted again overnight.
    Collective memories last in a short span of time before they
    are submerged into thick bleach and wiped away. The public
    does not have time to be woven into the maze of truth and
    untruth. The country is rushing to wealth; nobody wants
    to be missed out of this hype on the not-so-relevant pains of
    others.

13. I encountered estranged eyes when I mingled into the past.
    Acquaintances didn't want to discuss past incidents, or the
    level of absurdity was so overwhelming that it churned over
    their throats, and the dinner lost good tastes.
    Ones avoid facing it or having a conversation about it, or it is
    just an unwanted spice one doesn't want to add to their dinner
    plates. "Why do you bother? We cannot change anything?" a

journalist fellow asked me with repulsion, chewing a pork and scallion dim sum as if swallowing the stubborn past.

Since I stopped talking about the past, my life has become easier. No one complained. I didn't feel disappointed and blame others for their forgetfulness anymore. I preserve the past in its carcass bottle, opening it in the dark, smelling its pungent scent, its discreet existence bothering me, like the night in the hospital yard bothering me for years. Why were the front men of the glorious development killed in the front of prosperity? Who killed them?

14. The old woman I sat by that night appeared on TV. Hundreds of billions VND of donations poured into the village under the bridge, where all victims were from. Cash flows like the Hậu Giang River. Some officials handed her a hefty pile of cash. Her eyes squinted by the light of cameras and crowds. Her younger son died. The others were still in ER. They bought her sons' lives.

15. The present is national dementia. It requires one to note phases, date, times, and process to remember how a disaster happens. Those elements are crucial because they flow like the river, requiring a fluent narrative so that the fact is incorporated, the picture comprehended, the truth gradually forming like a jelly cake, despite being temporary, gaining some physical existence. Without a linear timeline, a disaster loses its coherence and quickly fades into the milky brain of collective dementia. The communist propaganda deploys sophisticated tactics to control the national memories: Never giving important things a proper definition, never letting the people form an attachment with a coherent story. Facts are stacked tight and shimmed with not-facts, mixed vigorously with rumors, conspiracies, and smears. Definitions are distorted in mocking names or soaked with humiliating jokes. The fusion brews a

pungent liquid; nobody wants to touch it. Too troubling and unpleasant.

16. For example:

Environmental activists are mocked as *prostitutes*.
Democracy is twisted into *cholera*.
Words stink.

17. Forming a detailed picture of how an event happened is an urge to keep my mind intact. I cut out newspaper reports from domestic and international news, compare them to each other, or compare them over important timelines. The comparison reveals hidden parts, sometimes revealing themselves like a cunning fox, sometimes hiding too well like snakes waiting for their prey among the dry leaves.

Then I arrange the process and compare it to the present presented. Another truth emerges like a bloating corpse on the river, out of everyone's consciousness and expectation, exposing itself like a shriek of an angry stork, flinging maggots into the air.

18. Then, the Japanese investors and construction contractors of Cần Thơ Bridge admitted they were too "hurried" to make the deck before building enough support parts for its weight.

Not the rain.

The humble-looking old men wearing expensive suits drove to Bình Minh Village with crews of national TV channels to say sorry for the victims' families. They shook hands with old mothers, bowing their heads many times on TV and in front of Vietnamese parents, who didn't understand what bowing meant or if it would return them their dead children.
The Japanese capitalists are good at it, hiding a sword to slit your stomach while gently smiling and bowing to your face. Then they announced a scholarship for all the orphans of dead workers. Then they resumed the construction. They called the project official development assistance loans from

the Japan Bank of International Cooperation to the Vietnamese government.

19. Even the past is disgusting. I keep staring at it, hoping it reveals itself and gives me more meaning to live and remain in my job. I was so immersed in my job that it became a part of me. I was miserable hoarding edited versions of the present. They clog my trachea, drawing oxygen out of my brain.

20. Two years after the dinner, that doctor was accused of sexual harassment of his patients.

21. I grew up breathing Buddhist air. Everyone I knew at the time practiced Buddhism in some way. My mother prayed for my well-being and did charity work to pay back to life. My friends prayed for me when they went to temples in Tết or in Hungry Ghost Month. My ex-boyfriend was a long-time follower of Buddhism. People I love and loved asked me to let go and not be attached too much because Buddha asks us to let go.

    Let go of what? If humans are not attached to anything, that being is not called human but a lifeless object. Are we attached to air? Do our lungs need air desperately every second to survive? Are we attached to water? Why do we go to war when we run out of water? Are we attached to other human beings? Should we ignore someone in an accident and walk away because we let go and don't attach? Do you consider looking away from victims of a bridge collapse as a manifestation of letting go or not being too attached?

    Let's face it, quoting a mantra of Buddhism is a way to hide oneself from the unpleasant realities of life, like the communists hiding the facts behind smearing words and adjusted truth. Convenient untruthfulness doesn't shield one from the crushing demonstration of injustice that others are suffering. It just covers one from one's own guilt of looking away from other people's pain.

22. Nobody was punished for their wrongdoings from the bridge collapse.

    If Buddha does that, that is his choice. Not mine.

23. Poet Osip Mandel'shtam wrote in his poem "The Horseshoe Finder":

    "What I am saying at this moment is not being said by me
    But is dug from the ground like grains of petrified wheat."
    ....
    "The century, trying to bite through them, left its teeth-marks
    there.
    Time pares me down like a coin,
    And there is no longer enough of me for myself."

    Mandel'shtam wrote and read this poem for some of his close friends before he was sentenced to several years' hard labor, dying in a transit camp en route to a gulag in the winter. The poem is remembered and recited among his friends until it finds another life elsewhere beyond the Soviet border.

    If not for his friends' memories, for their tight grip on a living piece of Mandel'shtam, I would never have a chance to read this poem.

24. The past can be fragmented, unpleasant, hurtful, or scary. But it doesn't mean we should bleach it white to the bones to feel pleasant.

    The past leaves its teeth marks in our lives like Mandel'shtam said, deep and bruised enough that I keep it like layers of blanket covering me through days and nights of negotiation with my own living among the collective dementia of Vietnam, rushing towards whatever is promising ahead in the price of those forsaken lives.

25. For the past is the cocoon of the present; staring at it can shield me from the restlessness of being in an absurd present, the motto of this century.

KARAOKE NIGHT IN CẦN THƠ

After "Real Karaoke People" by Ed-bok Lee

Do you hear her voice
hissing the moon tide
guiding dead soldiers home
holding his passed wife's hand?

A crude karaoke speaker:
a quiet god of sorrow
summons the tear river veering
to her home. Sing:

> *Mom, don't marry me off far from home*
> *And his grave lies next to hers*

Melancholic songs flood the screen
the shining bliss of life:
a wedding, a dragon festival, a river feast

In karaoke songs, young people die young
Wives lost husbands, mothers lost sons
until karaoke songs squirm in our chests
screamed their fates in entertainment

Everyone needs a karaoke stage
staging their sadness hiding
behind the curtains of joy
for the truth scratches our lungs

Sorrow evaporates
from kitchens, restaurants,
a lullaby, a blaring recitation:

> *Five brothers in a tank*
> *five flowers blooming on the same bush*

[we all know their tanks crushed through jungles and people flesh]

to lure the un-assurable
return to our demented homes
manifesting pains into quickened blasts

Our chests slit open
in the beat of karaoke songs
for homeless souls to leak in.

WATCHING FROM A SANDBANK

A blue dragonfly seeks
    a landing post.

    Summer ripes durians
    rambutan spins
    duckweeds

        into a ripple
        swallowing silt
        banks
        bloating a giant
        mud carp's ovary

            giving birth to
            rapids hissing through
            the sharp gills. Pumping

            Stirring the   island like
                    boiling tamarind
              soup   sprinkled
                    green
                scallions

Bamboo clumps
snap. Durians
    bounce. The dragonfly
        swerves
           into   an
             eddy
   A water strider
   glides when the island
   dissolves.

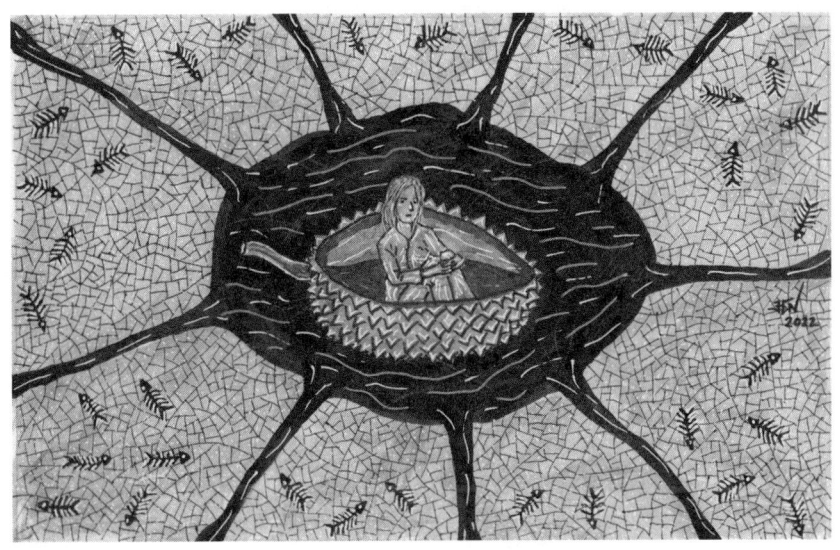

DAM INTO THE FUTURE

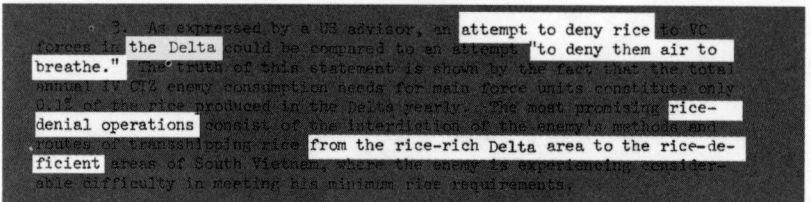

Report: **Rice in Vietnam** – *Combines Intelligence Center, 15 April 1969*
UNITED STATES MILITARY ASSISTANCE COMMAND, VIETNAM
Office of the Assistant Chief of Staff, Intelligence

Rice r
          a
          i
          n
          s
on the scalp
of a nation
uprooted
from old farmers' palms
brothers devour
harvests
in fratricidal banquets

          broken kernels
          germinate
          eyes
          in every rice bowl
             children chew

EROSION

Many years ago, my grandmother decided to stop living.

She lay in bed, refusing food and quietly drifting into her half-unconscious world. She didn't respond to any family members, including her husband and her sons. My mother was summoned to take care of her when the situation got worse. Mom caught a two-hour bus to her older brother's house, where my grandparents lived. They moved in with him six months before her self-starvation.

I knew about this time from my mother's words: Grandmother lay facing a white wall. She didn't want to turn back and see anyone.

Every morning, mom took off Grandmother's clothes, dipping the towel in warm water, scrubbing her skin, and changing her into a clean bathrobe. While doing that, my mom felt life was leaking out of the older woman's body. Her skin got ragged and lost flexibility. Her hair tangled like a hairball, although my mom combed it every morning. Her palm lay open; knuckles lost motion. Her limbs turned into heavy logs of their own weight, her lips a dry dike of sealed words.

When my grandmother was healthy and happy, she loved to be clean. She cleaned everything with passion, seeking dusty spots and wet marks and eliminating them in a blink, constantly sweeping the garden morning and late afternoon. When I visited her 20 years ago, she gave me a bath in half an hour, cleaning all my nails, my hair, and rubbing my skin until it turned red.

As a clean person gave up on her desire to live, it was the cleanliness that she gave up first. My mother stayed there two weeks, feeding her liquid congee, singing lullabies by her bed, talk-telling her old stories of the time she grew up. But my grandmother had already made up her mind. She died just a week after my mother left her.

***

My childhood memory had some sparks about my grandmother's house. It was a three-part house with six bedrooms in a shadowy alley, with coconut trees in front, a bell fruit tree bearing juicy fruit every summer, a pineapple garden behind, and all strangely postured bonsai trees belonging to my grandfather. There, I was attacked by bees when I tried to pluck a gloriously red bell fruit next to the hive. One season my grandpa showed me how he sculptured a deer out of bear's breech branches. But it was the humidity, the warm and fruit-scented air of the Mekong Delta, that made me yearn to return in summer, cocooning in its thick atmosphere, as if sweetness and textures of bursting mangoes, juicy pineapple, dropping coconuts, and clusters of longans marinated my skin and my hair in their generous growing pulses.

Then it became a garden of no return because I didn't get along with my relatives and never went back. Longing for the smell of home, I found another way to return to every garden in the Mekong Delta: I became a journalist. All farmers would love to have me around and show me how the swamp and muddy land blessed them with endless fruitful seasons.

After my grandmother refused to continue living, I went back to the delta more often, ruminating, welcoming a strange question coming to my awareness: how was one defined by one's home?

***

I visited Mrs. Hà Thị Bé's garden, located by word of mouth from people in the market. "Just walk straight until you see the water," a butcher pointed his knife toward a crumbling asphalt road, narrowing just enough for two motorbikes to pass each other.

"The floor broke in half." The grandmother in her 70s squinted her eyes, trying to measure up close how the horror happened just in a split moment. The white ceramic floor was separated, forming gnawing teeth. The house lay bare like the carcass of a giant animal, scattering sooty dented pots, a mini gas cooker, a wooden sofa, enormous rubble pile of wooden poles, concrete slabs, and aluminum toles reflecting the sunlight from the water.

That night, Bé was singing a lullaby for her grandson, Cò. She murmured the rhythm again, and I realized,

"O crane, where do you eat tonight
perching on soft branch falling in the pond?"

The crane in the folk song flew out in the dark, seeking food for her young, mistaking a soft branch for a sturdy branch, missing her footing, and drowning. In the last part of the song, she wailed for help and a fisherman saw her; she begged him to save her. In return, she swore to sacrifice her body for the man's bamboo shoot soup. She had him promise that if he cooked her, he would only use clean water, never murky water, because murky water broke her young's hearts.

Whenever listening to the song, I longed to ask the crane why she so cared about her children's wealth and dignity that the fisherman save her from drowning, but why didn't she care about her own life? But I stopped myself from asking Bé because her song was fractured when the wooden posts of her stilt house rubbed against metal and sang with her. Then aluminum toles shrieked desperately. The floor shivered. She tugged Cò into her arms and launched herself out of the house. In a jiffy, the earth roared, slowly getting lower and then exploding, waking all her neighbors up. Half of the floor and roof splintered into the water. White dust powdered the black night.

Cò whispered, "Grandma, if our house was dancing, that was when I knew we had to run, right?" "You are my smart little man." The little grandson clutched her leg. She stroked his hair, and I saw water in those transparent eye cones. When Bé stepped closer to the eroded edge, the boy held onto her leg, curiously looking down the steep patch of land. After examining it, he sat on her feet, gazing at a blue plastic toy car crushed into pieces below.

Survivors of land erosion responded slowly to the immediate reality. At first, if you asked them about their situation, they told you a vivid story with absolute calmness. Some, like Bé, went down to little details. She explained to me every minute, the last moment, the collapsed posture of wooden poles, which were swept, which were left, what she should have taken. She recited with eloquence as if it was someone else's tragedy, distant and unrelated to her.

Bé reminded me of my grandmother, her wrinkled eyes, generous smiles, dried and frail hands, and the little stooped posture. I wanted to know more about her life. "Do you remember how long you have lived here?" Bé went quiet, wandering in her head, trying to lift a foggy curtain of the past.

"Since I remembered, I have been here. My mom and I washed our clothes and washed dishes there since I was a little girl. My dad made a small pier from eucalyptus wood to anchor our boats. The river edge used to be over 300 meters behind our house." The pier disappeared a long time ago, together with a corn patch they grew for summer harvests. Nobody put on another dock on this side of the island, fearing that the river would consume anything growing. The spot that used to be Bé's home pier was now a calm water surface, reflecting the crisp blue sky in the delta as if there had never been a stretch of homes, land, or lives there. It was a void of an emptied memory that Bé couldn't hold up against time and the massive erosion.

There lay two soot-coated pots twisted on top of broken ceramic pieces and cement chunks. They were remnants of a disrupted warm-hearted kitchen. Island people used to be so poor that they started home with cooking pots, a symbolic object of a fulfilling future. Bé's mother gave them to her nearly 40 years ago at the time of her marriage. The pots had served her family since her husband was alive, and through the births of their three children. She had cooked a farewell dinner with the same pots when her husband passed away and cooked the first meal to welcome the daughter-in-law, Cò's mother, into the family.

Now the utensils' bottoms were torn amid the rubble, unable to bless Bé by her mother's words.

***

When my grandparents bought their house in the Mekong Delta, they realized their dream of wealth in the opening economy. Before it, they lived in communal housing or company housing, depending on my grandfather's job. Having a house with six bedrooms for all their grown-up children was a contented dream. My grandparents achieved that with years of growing and trading fruits from their small farm. They insisted that we visited every Tết holiday because they had enough space for all their kids to be together like in the old days.

The Mekong Delta was a land of generosity. My grandmother told me that if you accidentally spit out a papaya seed, the delta gives you a fruit-laden papaya tree. The heavily alluvial water flew from Tibet, down to Myanmar, Thailand, Laos, Cambodia, and ended up in the Mekong Delta, where the abundance landed on the muddy feet of Mekong farmers. We never thought of things like "food security" because we were the country's food security. We grew enough rice for Vietnam to feed the world. Maybe one day in the supermarket, you would recognize the rice from the Mekong Delta that you serve in your dinner grown from some unknown rice field like my grandparents'. In summer, I slept on a hammock strung between two mango trees. I dreamt of mango growing out of my palms, exquisitely tangy and sweet. I heard jackfruits cracking open and indulged in their heavenly smell.

***

Years ago, I went to Sa Đéc, the flower capital of the delta, and walked into the flower district in late afternoon. A woman asked me where I was heading to. I told her I wanted to smell flowers. "Go to my place, we have a spare bed, you can sleep, you can go see the garden tomorrow." I followed her home. Her house was a flower and frog farm, floating halfway out of the river's edge. I opened the window from my bed and smelled the slightly pungent mud mixed with marigold. The frogs gossiped to the moon, disrupting my sleep in which marigolds quietly laughed beside my shins, crossing and touching their leaves.

In the morning, the flower farm woman told me that her village had grown flowers for generations, six or seven, she couldn't tell, but she grew up with acres of apricots, water lilies, and marigolds, as in her grandparents' time. When the flood season came, they moved flower-pots to bamboo shelves built upon water level to not let them drown.

Suddenly those gardens returned to my head when Bé walked me through her disappeared home garden toward the river edge. The smooth asphalt road rose up and concaved down into shallow holes and rugged paths. The asphalt broke like rice crackers into black bitumen chunks on jagged edges. The road ended abruptly on a steep drop, exposing layers of the earth's flesh. "Some years ago, this used to be the main road of our village," Bé described while chopping at giant grass to make way for us through an alternate path to her used-to-be garden.

The swift rapid had been gnawing on roads and pulled houses one by one into the river on many secretive nights. Bé's house was just one of over a hundred unlucky ones ending in the same riverbed. Under giant grass bush, my feet felt the slippery surface of ceramic tiles and cement floors. It used to be the homes of someone, of many people who drifted away when their village eroded into the river. Bé used to harvest corn now and then and grilled corn with fried scallion. She would sit in front of the house and turn fresh corn on top of glowing charcoals for her grandchildren when they finished school and dropped by her house for snacks. She grew morning glory, mustard greens, okra, sponge gourd, and bitter gourd every season. She kept listing the names of them because memories flooded out of her mouth and vaporized into this devastating wreckage. She couldn't stop; I couldn't catch all of them.

A small clay Earth God sat discreetly in the bush in the middle of the grass-covered patch with his enormous wealthy laugh. Some house owners forgot him when they ran for their lives. Bé picked him up, putting him on a clean tiled spot, rubbing muddy spots off his ceramic feet and genuflecting to him with prayers.

Bé's new house was built in a resettlement area in the middle of the island, about 1.2 miles from the corroded site. Since they moved in, Cò would wake up around midnight, sobbing quietly, holding his grandma's arm tight, anchoring himself on a safe foundation he had lost. Then he gradually drifted back to far-flung dreams behind closed eyelids when grandma whispered a lullaby by his ears.

Since the erosion, Cò insisted Bé take him to the riverbank after school for months after the house faded. He wanted to walk on the same path "home" until he reached the broken edges and watched the falling scaffolds and the rubble sink deeper into the water. He stared down the edge, then quietly pulled his grandma's hands and they left together, leaving the home alone for another night.

"I miss being here. At night the water burbled through the sandbank. Now we live on the main street. I have to listen to young people race their bikes through noisy pipes. The smell of gas. Sound of engines. I can't sleep." Bé moved her shoulders as if she was struggling in an invisible suit, a new house suffocating her.

"Your grandmother asked me if you still remember the red bell fruit tree. I thought she lost her mind." My mother called me in the middle of her last care-taking trip to my uncle's home. I could hear the roaring engines of container trucks screeching on the highway in the background. Living in Saigon was living in the concrete jungle and a swamp of industrial noise.

I didn't take her description of my grandmother seriously, thinking old people had their own uncomfortable clutch to hang onto with intense disapproval and nastiness. Once grandma got angry with me when I accidentally broke the pottery jar that she used to preserve yeasts to make bread. She kept many beautiful metal tea boxes, with Chinese poems carved sophisticatedly next to white-bearded men and storks. She wore a faux emerald pearl on her neck for years because it reminded her of her mother. Now Bé told me that she missed the water burbling. I didn't understand that the disruption of surroundings could wreck their lives. One's life was defined by the beloving air, the sound, the vegetables they grow, the spices and herbs they harvested, the land and mud touching their feet. Their lives were the land's life itself. Detaching them from land was cutting nutrition from a growing fetus in its mother's womb. What did my grandmother yearn for? Did she keep returning to her sweet bell fruit tree until her breath exhausted?

I stood next to Bé, crouching by a slaughtered wall with a window frame looking out at the horizon. The broken house window framed a losing past and an uncertain present no longer co-existing with the Mekong as their ancestors used to do. The horizon behind the window was disrupted by giant metal arms of sand dredgers, clear-cutting the landscapes into fragments. They were gutting the river leisurely in hums of engines, every season, every day for years and years to come.

Hồng Ngự, Bé's hometown, was the sand capital of the Mekong Delta. The sand was liquid gold, simply scraped off the riverbed, dried up on immense metal barges, and transported through the network of rivers to anywhere thirsty for development, from Saigon to Singapore, Dubai, or Hong Kong, erecting skyscrapers that we saw in blockbusters like *Crazy Rich Asians*. None of these glamorous financial buildings and theme parks devoted space to illustrating houses committing suicide in the river. People of the developed worlds admired Asia getting rich; I counted tiny villages and islands sacrificing themselves for that pride. It was as if you were watching an irony in operation.

***

I walked around the same village, seeking to talk to a sand miner. Old grandparents in the area disapproved of the idea, saying they were violent and distant, hostile outsiders. From afar, dark-skinned men walked and shoveled on barges floating lazily on the water. There was no sound. They worked persistently like an army of ants, moving mountains to mountains, rivers to rivers, looting islands' foundations discreetly. Rarely did I see any of them look up or look toward me on the riverside. No eye contacts.

A tall man in the market invited me to his home because he claimed to know the story about sand miners.

"I was a sand miner." Thành poured hot tea in a white ceramic cup and pushed it toward me. His house was well built with good-quality wood and new aluminum toles. Behind the house, there were a fish farm and a duck farm. We talked among the busy quacking ducks.

Thành became a sand miner because his father's farm eroded completely. He had no land and no job. His fellows said he just needed a pump, and he could make a living. Thành went out every night on his wooden sampan run by a small Yamaha boat engine. He dropped a pipe into the water and pumped sand up to the boat. He rode to the sand wholesalers and sold it for over 10 million VNĐ (~500 USD) by morning. He and his sister became sand miners like that and worked thus for years, earning the amount of cash that no farmer could realize in their lifetime.

"I quit when my mother got cancer. I want to stay at home more and take care of her. I grow fish and duck now." Thành finished his monologue, and I wriggled on my chair, not knowing what to ask. "I think it is karma. My mother is paying for what I did." Thành sipped the tea, and his eyes squinted because the sun was too bright on the river. Sand miners knew what they caused, but it was quiet reasoning among them that they worked for a living, munching their motherland for food. Thành turned from a firsthand victim to a perpetrator himself. He and his neighbors didn't talk to each other. It was everyone else's business that the island corroded.

"We gathered the villagers to chase [the sand miners] away. We filed lawsuits against them. They just went about their business because nothing could harm them. Our house eroded. We were too busy to take care of our homes. People moved away when their houses collapsed." Bé described the cycle, which explained the dynamic between houseless farmers and sand miners. Environmentalists at Cần Thơ University found giant water holes underneath sand mines in the river. They created a stronger water flow. Hence, rapids "chewed" on both riversides where alluvium and silt are soft, sweeping the land away in its path. Local government asserted that the holes were natural. Naturally, like that, Bé and her neighbors turned into refugees on their fatherland.

***

Bé's island lay by the same river near my grandmother's garden. Mekong people said that we all were born from water and dissolved into water.

My grandmother didn't fulfill that prophecy of the land. Before setting herself to starve, she discovered that her son, Mom's older brother, sold her land and her house to pay his debt. "She missed her home," Mom explained, as if it was a justifiable reason to die. My grandmother was uprooted to Saigon and buried in an urban graveyard somewhere I had never visited. She didn't dissolve into water. Could one abandon one's life for the sake of a piece of land? Does anyone out there do that?

Bé was uprooted from her riverbank. She had a small ledger for years now to keep account of the housing expenses. She could see her resettling house was draining them up in a frightening new life. Her finger moved along a new column of spending, shaking quietly with things like a fan, water usage, gasoline, electricity. . . . She didn't buy a fan before because her house was full of breeze and rice-scented air. She didn't pay for water; a small well provided, and she washed all the clothes in the river. No motorbike was needed; they lived by the market and a ferry. She walked with a basket to sell fruits and bring food home. Suddenly, everything cost.

***

In the very last days of my grandmother, she changed her side toward my mother. It was easier to clean and to help her sit up. Tears came from her eyes while my mother was wiping her face and neck. She exhaled, and her shoulders trembled. My mother sat closer to her and hugged her. "She was leaving." My mother admitted her caring couldn't pull my grandmother back from her path. She had no home to which to return; better leaving the unbearable noise of the city wrapped up in its chaos.

But "leaving" was a privilege for those who had a place to leave and return to, like my grandmother. One left only when there was a place to depart, a ferry, a bus station, a home. If one's home disappeared, one was abandoned in the void, disoriented and disgraced. One didn't know where to begin or to continue. There was nowhere to start again.

Bé led me through the path cut into a busy village market. Nearby, some houses were abandoned. Two graves lay cold in front, no incense, no flowers. Mekong people used to bury their ancestors in the garden to continue their next lives close to their grandchildren, watching descendants thrive. Bé whispered to me: "They were my parents' friends. Their children left. All their rice fields and garden went into the water some years ago."

I wonder how long these two graves would still stay with their grandchildren. Would they still be here when the children come back?

The living have no home to return to; the dead waited for the river to call them in some random night corrosion.

DEAR HẬU GIANG,

Before your flesh was excavated,
you combed my hair. Now
picking up your bones, I see hair
tangled underneath.

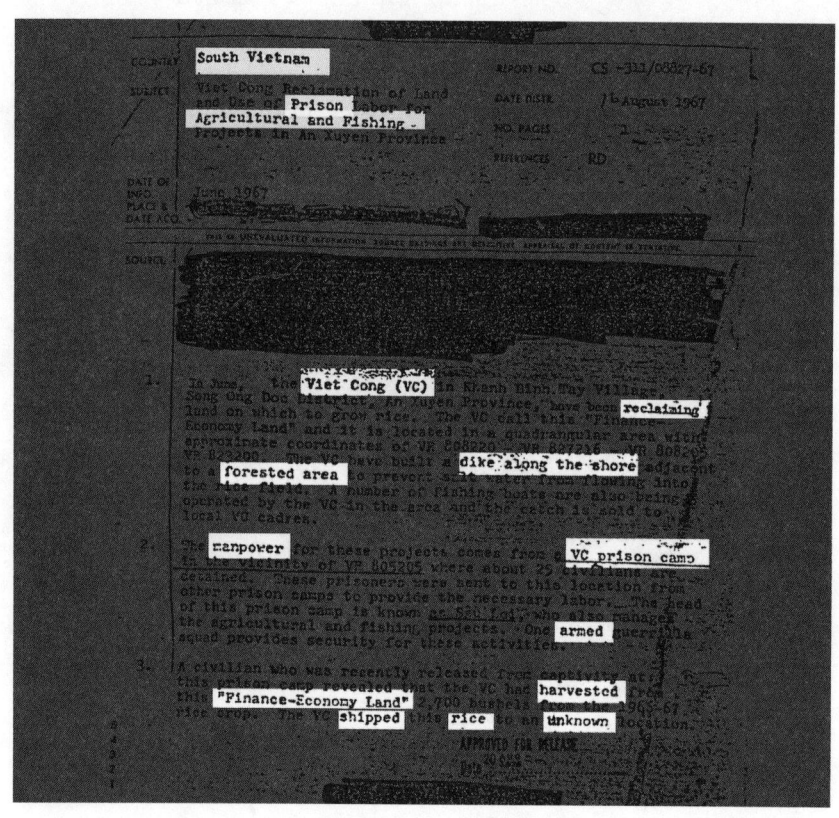

CIA – Intelligence Information Cable
Country – South Vietnam
DOI – June 1967
Report No – CS-311/08827-67

HUNGER SEASON

The straw shed cast a shadow on rotten
soils. The daughter gazed at   gnawing
teeth -   rumbling concrete banks
Her heels peeled off the sand

Hungry souls wandered on ripples
tears on the lost dwellings
The wind swept by failing gardens
Slithering wounds.

From wars to famines
The dying flecks shone
                        over cold rice
Hundred-year-shadows
            vanished; the soil evanesced

Ancestors walked like paper   puppets
mourning their missing children
pierced by fired bullets
                    [in an   erased war].

The girl munched dead kernels
Hunger thinned her
into a paper   cutout, taped
                                on a corroded wall.
Milky seedlings tasted   salty.

THE ISLAND DECIDES TO DISAPPEAR

from the other side of the Mekong River
I bury my face in a vague prayer
It was only a nightmare
soon passing by

A grandmother washes clothes by the wooden bridge
Her daughter sings a lullaby
the stilt house swings on lanky acacia legs
Slow rapids lick the edge of soil
tear the dirt road apart

The fisherman boasts a great catch
Silver fish play in the fertile flood
Crossing the river tonight
they would become delicate sour hotpots
in the early morning market
I brush off the exotic imagination
because asphalt roads are cracking like rice cakes

The turbulence of dust
coughed out the chest pain
of a thousand-year-old man

A flock of children plunge into the alluvial body
Playing hide and seek in hugs of Mother River
They laugh and holler in the gloaming
Where have they left?

The island dives
like the legendary giant catfish,
thrashing its body
hides in the water hole of extinction

Silence shrouds.

A folk song picked up by wind
spilling on the ripples
"If you leave the village to marry someone
I would wait here every night; the river breeze brings your hair scent home"
After tonight, no shore to anchor the loving breeze

The island trembles
shrugging off hundreds of years of existence

Night is dense and warm
Why are my palms chilly?

EVERY YEAR GROWS MORE BITTER

Rain eats water
Soil dismantles land

In Bến Tre, coconut thirsts
Bạc Liêu sea creeps in
An Giang burns rice into billowing ash.

Everywhere else, people eat Mekong rice.

Import	unrooted	degenerate
Hunger	dry mouths	wander
Export	spraying	mutated
Wealth	spread	forgetfulness

On TV, an old farmer wept, "I lost everything."

in the beginning of the end of the beginning of
        the end of the beginning of the end of the *rice-bowl region*.

ARID DELTA

A rice plant feeds me young
grains. My feet take
root on the barren dirt. Cracked
heel. Bleed. Seedlings suck
my liquid – but a water
buffalo strikes. The field
falls by its hooves. The Earth opens
its chest. My half body
sinks. The buffalo whistles a song – *Pull
me* – Her song molds my parents
in silt and straw. Parents soak
me in the flood. I squeeze
the buffalo's horn. She gores
parents. They disperse into
herons. Orphan. I snug
into the buffalo's arms. Enwind.
My palms hold her hooves. The sky turns
river. Earth vomits. Herons
are drowned. My cracked heels
devour silt. The sun tips the river
over. If I sink into the buffalo's belly,
I grab her umbilical
cord. If I drink her milk, earth
cannot swallow me. I break
the cycle. Dry feet. Dead rice.

WATER SONNET

Drink this water from the highest mountains
Splitting glaciers and feeding mangoes
This water diffuses Tibetan monks' ash
from their self-immolation yearning return
Drink this water, taste those scattered from home
in the cursing power of our shining Buddha
Gulp this water diluting temple's smoke
mourning Vientiane sky, Thais' stampeding elephants
May Buddha melt on fire on flesh on killing fields
His lips swallows the bleeding Tonlé Sap
The land the sun never sets all summers
Borders sketches his fraudulent smirks
Now drown in water where Buddha betrays---
Concrete dams choke the way to oceans.

FEARING THE DAMS SUCKING OUT THE MEKONG'S SOUL

I stuff my mouth with alluvium,
the gray soil tinged my grandparents' breath
dissolving generations of rice beds,
rice kernels; burning piles of quiet bodies
laughing with their loud-gaping skulls
under swamps. The mythical giant catfish slip through borders
sneaking in - sneaking out - sneaking
into the chants of old monks, blinded by the buzzing
Chinooks, evaporating into gray clouds of giant mosquitoes.
Pungent. Greedy as I am, fearing the delta cannibalizing
itself in the hungry water, I swallow the dirt rising in my throat
until a scream breaks out into an October flood.
My home -- coconut thatch shredded,
its scaffoldings let go,

> the remnant of my childhood spilling out
> unrestrainable

I call names – my beloveds
My tongue is gagged by gravel. No one
replies. Sediment

> .rises.
> . Sucked. Unrestrainable.

SAND DUNE

The dune bloats like fuming pimples on the
Moon, from the gutted riverbed

The boy climbs on and slides down
into the river carcass

Last night dredgers slung metallic arms
groping the beating heart of the Mekong

Their steel claws gouged until dawn
The morning dew fell into the starving water

The river moos like a wounded buffalo
swallows emptiness

A whirlpool gobbles a paddy field
spitting out murky flux

From the dune top

The boy watches his mother leave home
When the rice field dried in anguish

His father rows a boat and faded
where the river meets the sea; overturned

the dune heaves on the river chest
a vessel of revenge.

ORIGIN OF DAMS

I lie down by a rice plant. Her neighbors dance on the wave of wind,
from the North where alluvium crossed the

threshold of D-   D-   D-
      -A- from Tibet   -A-   - A -
      -M-   -M- crash on Laos   -M -
        -S-   -S-   - S
                                              - suck Tonlé Sap

My nails dig in her roots. Curling up, she seeks the taste of living. But
what she finds hurts her. Squeezed throat. I gasp her name. She spins
a root into my ears, searching my beats and cells. My face sinks in the
muddy field, listening to her pulses growing out of my brain sutures.
My temples hymn an ancient song of starving mothers drowned in
soldiers' onslaught. Her threads multiplied in my lungs, my burning
jungle, my river of veins, my peeling heel skin.
My heart beats
               salty
          intoxicating water
            licking — the sea
                — bittersweet —
                    Whitening — bust — to dust

                      untangling her
                      untangling me
                      untangling our land.

AN ASSURANCE ON SEA RISING

Recently, I have been listening
the Mekong soil spasms under my feet

I don't want to die in a restless erosion,
crunching Bạc Liêu coast in highway hysteria crashes

Yet I don't want to live in a serene blindness
sinking my teeth in a bleeding pomelo

while their roots spit out salt
the century rises ocean on their tips

I don't want to ride a boat on an empty river
filled with my ancestors' crimes

I want to stand by the exhausted bamboo shoots
the delta kisses, a breeze scents rice flowers

I want to cuddle floating duckweeds
tiny leaves brush my aroused curly hair

I want to sleep in a fluffy swampland
floating on the lover's chest - the heaving field

Maybe I could hear the Mekong's beat,
countdowns our existence, relentless joys.

DROWNING DRAGON*

I snake through jungles in the black morning
The cunning crocodile cackles between teeth
Faceless bodies dropped from the land above
dropping into his mouth - a feast of lies
He spends the dawn ripping flesh apart
saving for years of gods' upheaval.

I am a rice germ – reaped out in milling
execution, trashed from abundant meals
The sickening sun rises in the pesticide odor
cursing seasons of wealth - endless
rice bowls until poisoned.

I am a water hyacinth - a dark prophet
rooting in the lurking Sun
by a mother's boat; paddles in her hand
dividing water and dry riverbed
conceiving an abandoned land.

I am a neglected child - the sacrifice
for abundance - diked into thousands of canals,
creeks, irrigating my veins into the sediment
banks. My mouth swells in
spices of fertilizers — liquid metal.

---

*Cửu Long aka Nine Dragons aka Mekong Delta.

I am a dragon, yet ones think of me otherwise
My body: extraction of cheap — — lives,
naive abundance — exploited rice
bowl — — Here I am — scaled and
sunk — into the

— sea ——
————

—

A FABLE OF RICE

1.

Gliding there invisible graves
       between the river's gut
Fluttering there mourning songs
           once lovers' wine spilled
Opening there scars on grandfather's arms
               slashed by the century of sickles and hammers
Forgotten there the giant barb
         slipping into black sinkholes
The land of rice eats the rice kin

2.

: our exotic land
      hairy jungles curvy rims
: Marguerite Duras' *Lover* colonial-styled fucks *Indochina's*
      fables of arousing nipples
      creamy coconut milk
         drips into white men's teeth
         sucking abundant breasts
         starving women
         assembed forced smiles
         too white to be seen
   too white erasing the land too white
      white too white too white too

3.

    : brushstrokes of massacres
                executions   ~~erased~~
              theme parks of erotica un^{headed} bodies
        on polished white magazines:
                    trendy   barbaric
The charming *bà ba* rides a leafy boat   black hems smirk with murderers

4.

The flattering Gray Suit stands in front of Buddha
                          Master's mother's home
His souvenir picture: *a tour to Nam*
His brags by BBQ on The 4th of July:
              adventures   into morality of yellow fever
He gives guns to Buddha's adherents
              hypnotizing: his Jesus and
                        flesh gods – who die first?
Because M14 can blow holes
    The demon   waves to assassin gods
                    of others

5.

then Buddha Master was killed
              the delta consumes him and others
            into abundance
                talks-stories dissolved

6.

O mother, your boat divides water
You paddled loving strokes
You blinked at my father on the river edge
begetting me from the seeds of tamarind

touch me, my skin is sawdust
          O mother, are we thirsty?

cuddle my hair, don't mistake me with beheaded fish
          lying bare on your cutting board

feed me your rice, feed me until choked
          O mother, I am rising like smoke
            a hungry ghost losing her mind
my hand, my cracking skin,
        born from your womb, feed myself for alluvium
                river sprouting
                  rice.

FLYING DREAM OF THE MEKONG'S CHILD

That night and some nights on
I slept by her in our land's brothel
Her bed, thousand men's sweat soaked
in pursuit of her rising hips

But the night was licking its wounds
to cover liquid marks in lemongrass
dripping from her hair, bathing her.

In the morning, she leaves a *bánh mì*
on the dampened couch
I chewed the crispy roasted pork skin
spurring scent of desire ghosts

At noon she asked me to get out
customers yearn for her singing nipples
Her pale skin: the land of misty soil
mounting their hard-ons until blistered

I sat by the babbling sewage
fuming in spilling bubbles
Her utter of pleasure vaporizes
the men oinked

Twilight sat on a soggy blanket
Saigon sparkled between her matted hairs
jungle of softness, ocean rising
a blind dragon stumbles by dead mangrove forest.

Again, the night drops saliva on my palm
I retreated to her field, a hermit crab
shell, whistling to far-flung oceans,
she pulled me onto the dragon's back.

DAMMING

I bought a bamboo lamp in a flea market by the river edge. It bent towards the seller like an obsequious slave waiting to be bargained. The old Thai vendor told me to take it and give him whatever I pleased. He wanted to leave quick. Before the water rose. Before riverweed died.

The lamp skeleton was coated in white paint, as smooth as a young woman's skin. I turned on the temperamental switch. The bulb gazed straight at my eye cones, as if trying to split me open with the arrogant brightness. It reached for the black matter inside me, calling for a water surge. Outside the window, the river was gorging secret sinkholes. I turned the light off, a storm coming, dams grumbling afar.

The lamp observed my face like an assiduous superior. My left temple twitched when I jotted down a conspiracy to break through a dam construction site. Fishermen did that when their fish were massacred by the power station. Some C-4. Ambushing excavators. Landfall. The lamp pinned its eyes at my crossed-out words. It blazed the letters under the white dome draping from high, subduing me in a foggy oblivion. My right temple heard the concrete bank unravel.

The lamp's glare didn't leave my dreams alone. An old woman secretly bred fish under her skirt. She walked on the water's surface, spreading seeds like shedding feathers at twilight. Tiny fish swam out into underwater rainbows. The Mekong breathed in fish clouds, breathed out giant barbs. Tiny people marching out on my forehead, setting up a directed blasting, counting 3 2 1 and a gigantic waterfall burst, rock tattering in the air. A new dam was formed. Her tiny infants were muddled up in particles. The lamp watching me up close, waiting for my sutures torn apart to examine if it was worth it to blow me apart. Electricity ran in its throat, sucking the river out.

One night I was sexting with a colleague; he wanted to flood me with his semen, seasonal mating frenzy on Tonlé Sap. Mud carp, snakehead, walking catfish, featherbacks swam into his liquid pipe. I was panting. My hand touched my wetness. My eyes scanned the lamp, the only naked witness in front of me. O River this pleasure. Did the electricity become too strong, or the lamp smirk at me with a blind spark? I slipped the phone under my thighs, hiding the burning desire of being filled and flooded like a thirsty silver barb, getting dried in a blanket of lonesome. I, a thirsty suckermouth fish lay bare, humiliated and pleasured.

The lamp didn't hide its conspiracy against me. I had a water lily pot from an old woman in the village. She said if the buds bloomed purple, my barren lungs would be moist again. I promised to take care of the plant. Two buds fluttered like tiny smiles. The murder happened when I was away. My absence blew the dust wind into the window. The lamp spiked cruel light, draining life out of the innocent buds. Their souls left in a strip of smoke. When I returned, the cold light froze my fingers. The lamp bent at the shedding buds; its mouth was chomping the stillbirth roots. Its insidious bulb leered at me.

A bag of rice was sent to me. A tiny rice weevil climbed out. It looked up and dug a hole to hide. I got mad and searched it out among the ocean of tiny round grains. I took the lamp and put my face up close to the rice bag, digging at the spot where the weevil disappeared. Rice smelled the sweetness of a lost childhood, young grain heaven floating on its own milk. The lamp pushed my head lower into that misty haze. I dove in. My back was boneless. My upper body wriggled as the lower body lost its capability to obey my brain. The dirty wooden floor was scattered with my shedding hair.

This time the lamp pushed me down. My nostrils filled with rice, rice leaking into my lungs, rice flooding my gums, my throat. The electrical laughter drilled my ears until some liquid surged like a dam break. River dolphins swam out, side by side with giant catfish, towards the old woman walking on water.

MATCHMAKING

—For 70,000 foreign brides from the Delta

She went out and sought a husband

In the matchmaker's album, her eyes watered
a garden: mango flowers bloomed
on black soil, her sisters indulged
sweetening Korean dramas

Her hands cupped secret lotus buds
they would bloom on hardened snow
of far northern land, in the heart of
a man bought out her roots.

Her fingers wove a rope through oceans to
him. The matchmaker lady, neck sparkling with gold
chain, unraveled her yearning knots, calculated
50% commission of hope.

Her photo smiled at
an empty shell: face unknown, hand
untouched. She swept sweat on rice fields
The Sun cringed by her hip bones

One day a man from a far-away land came
I saw her on TV: lotus buds covered, pixelated
face, chest blanketed in rags. Headlines:
"Mekong brides faking blind dates,

slept with men in police raid."
TV watchers slurped in the frenzy
her dare to seek air beyond suffocation
I drank her naked garden on screen.

Years after on her island, the man
roped from the unknown sea, kissing
her forehead, lifting a baby on his shoulders
he speaks the language of *kimchi*, salt fish

Potent chili adorns her lips
He married her after they were detained
He didn't know blind dates
were crimes, so he decided to love

the criminal bearing
a mango garden on snow.

MOON SEASON

I was born in an erosion
sucking milk off my mom's fingertip

Years later, I watch a temple glide
when it dips a toe in the river

I scratch the leafroller's belly
folding the horizon in its fragile vessel

I beg durian flesh glorious yellow
for mom to soak her teeth in a silky treat

But Mom spits out empty rice brans
drowned in the dragonfly's eyes

The sky loomed in a plague of locusts
white cranes get drunk in a feeding frenzy.

All of these happen when the monk slips
because he walks out to admire the moon

                          eroding with his temple.

COMMODITY

In 2014, a major online newspaper in Vietnam ran a headline:
"Gái miền Tây và 3 chữ "N" nổi danh thiên hạ"
[Mekong Delta Women and Their Three Notoriously Famous "N"],
which are "ngon, ngoan, ngu" [juicy, obedient, and stupid].

The mother crosses Tiền Giang
On her back, the horizon rises smoke

The rice brans broke in half
Filling her sky with anguished flying bulbuls

Tearing their lungs in dry screams
Rushes for the shadow of her streaming hair

She carries her daughters' eyes
the dimming light in drought nights

Hunger hangs on a thread, dangling
fear cracks from the calloused soil

Her shadow frays in a dizzy sweatshop
hope numbs into stitches of shoes

Thousands of her kind
drain their youth in the filmsy reality

On shoe sole patching chains
In garment assembly lines

In the tombstone of Nike factories
Juicy, obedient, stupid

In the collective exploitation
She, a commodity ----

[On TV] She returns home, hands loads of cash
successful women reconstruct their hometown

[otherwise] she evaporates
[this is not reported].[not reported]

FOREIGN HUSBANDS

*"For Some in Vietnam, Prosperity
Is a South Korean Son-in-Law"*
—*New York Times, March 12, 2012*

The blushing brides shy away from guests at
weddings—which promised new houses to
their impoverished parents—they show us money cannot buy
happiness even though they starve from drought and crop
failures. We chant om in yoga poses munching
imported almonds and keto meal plans, dropping
fat from outsized waists, symptom of wealth.
The brides relieve their parents' hunger—offering themselves
to foreign husbands in catalogues—who do not even speak the same
language,
no courting, no love; we scoff. We got married to the husbands
devoted to homes, where they returned, wrecked
on whiskey—lipstick on their necks
Our sons shrugged—obsolete mothers perturbing their lives;
by then, we post contented family
pictures assuring our wholesomeness,
not like those brides selling their bodies.
If I were a farmer's daughter, an incubus of hunger of Mekong
I had scavenged dusty fields and depleted rivers for jasmine
rice and fresh tilapia, if I could mix papaya salad
in our decayed stilt home, I would marry a husband of the
same language and we'd insult each other for
the rest of our lives in our mother tongue.

"WHERE GIRLS ARE CHEAPER THAN AIR CONDITIONERS" [EAVESDROPPING WHITE TOURISTS IN A BACKPACKER HOSTEL IN PHNOM PENH]

is where white tourists strolling by Buddha's closing
eyes and grabbing a kid's growing breasts
here human dignity cannot afford a *fish amok*

is where they talk about "the world," meaning the meager
part of Cambodia bending its back
to be tagged on branded shoes and bags
reek of praises and glamor in Milan

is where they talk about saving the ocean
meaning exporting plastic mountains
floating them in the Pacific of Indonesia

is where they talk about reducing emissions
meaning choking the Amazon
in carbon offset harvest

is where ocean swallows dumpster
DDT tanks marinates seabed
Aspiring neodymium mountains
glittering in e-vehicle organs.

Here on Earth is where girls are cheaper than air conditioners

EDUCATED

My mother cut off a mud carp head, its body bathing in tamarind
leaves, billowing bitter herb, floating pineapple. Lilies bloom in the
fish's mouth, eye cones dimming light on my spelling lessons, the iris
outpouring the Mekong water my classmates jump into joys. Then
our elementary class spiked into the fish bones, when teachers' words
penetrated my mom's cheeks: *Why do you never pay the tuition fee?*

Words string tears up, a pearl necklace for every illiterate kid, sinking
in the muddy soup. Acrid. Mekong River sprawls its thousands of
arms, pumping breath to the gaping mouths, pumping the fish's
heart a stream of rushing joy. Mom's eyes melt into the boiling pot,
praying Buddha for me to sprout like rice & water hyacinth & grass
& duckweed & elephant ears & scallion & banana flowers & riverbed
alluvium. To outdrink the thirst of Mekong.

The mud carp's heart was

      beating

in the tamarind water

sour the sweating sun

              sour the lotus roots
          sour bamboo bushes
                    sour gourd vines
             sour clams' lips
sour my mom's
          tongue

sour my   scales
                    gills

               eyes

sour lessons beating up my head
math problems sprout faux promises
my teacher stares at me:
a mud carp never leaves her muddy field

SINKING TOWN

For Sài Gòn

A boy was sucked into the sewage
My boyfriend mentioned leisurely
                              sprinkling green
                                    onion on my congee bowl
The rain drums on glass windows
pecking like angry crows
the spring onion carries me back to the afternoon:
an old woman pulled my bicycle out of a black
                                    water   hole   pulling
                                    at the junction
A screw on the pedal cut my arm – bleeding
I might have joined him, a voice whispers in my head

Next morning I walk into
the fever of water
in fruit vendors' gossip:
                    High tide in   midtown
                    bananas,   guavas   coconut floating
                              waves surged onto buses
Fish net in hand, they caught mangosteens drifting wild
They missed some watermelons
                    swimming fastest since *Mai An Tiêm's* century -
The Watermelon Prince threw into the ocean
aching for the motherland
                    abandoning him

The fever sways me in
where boys and girls are pulled down
the tidal flood

I lift every sewage covers
                              broken   drainage pipes
In despair seeking for innocent arms
                                        hanging
                                        down
                                        there
Sewers grow to a   black ocean
                                      cutting
                                      the district from   its
                                              city -   island
                                      at   midtown
I see me – stepping
                  into
                  a pothole
                        into a drowning town
Rapids of
                  sponge white boxes
                        red coke bottles
                  laughing shampoo packages
                              breathing to the river mouth
                              in the destined hundred-year flood

I --- the tiny Noah in the
                  trash ocean.

PROPAGANDA ABOUT EDUCATION FOR IMPOVERISHED GIRLS

They smiled on newspapers
those made it to the camera light

Down here, between coconut tree legs
young girls were buried

in their ingredients of hope:
white papers, purple inks - education

sharpened pencils
sketching the thrashing land

bureaucratic officials chew
better future with sweet rice

Every morning young girls walked to school
chirping with birds slipping by fish

they illustrate a future
laid upon them on glossy papers

cold as razors, splitting their finger in half
from inside, they saw their truer

        talking them into gardens of desperation

we all know that our hope reeks
we strangle them like we strangle our kin

we squeeze young hair slender cheeks
to water our overcropped land

We mimic the chatter of liar storks
On TV: *Every girl should go to school*

But there is no school for their strayed feet.

ÁO BÀ BA IN PHỞ RESTAURANT

In a phở restaurant in San José hung a painting
a young woman in pink *bà ba*,
hems flapping, sweet breeze
the sun creamy like sugar cane foam

Her sampan: flirting with water hyacinth.
Paddles circle me to the delta she stood
An old grandmother, giggling on noodle boat
feeding children crossing water for school

A young mom breastfeeds her little lotus
a lullaby cushions sleeping cheeks
The morning market buzzes lyrical cries
Pineapple eyes squint at the gleaming morning

By her gaze on the walled –
noodle house I am chewing beef
observing her – my other self – discarded:
We stand in the muddled past

The dusty present covers her in
withering lotus; seawater flirts
rice paddies, licking her feet
until bitter salt penetrates her heels

I looked down my feet on the blazing
white ceramic floor, toes covered
in invisible mud, the pungent clay
coating my past in a fragile cell

That home I shredded behind, begetting
me – in this fashion of loss:
The filmsy canvas nails us
in the foreign decoration of prosperity.

FISH-ING

When your mother created us a home
she did not know we would bury her
at the same horizon

The boat lurked in thickets
water hyacinths crushed purple
eyes - bruises on my bones.

Your mother handed you to
me; her arms dangled
the river bled soft

I dared not search for her
in your eyes
blinks of longing

Your tiny fingers patted
morning glory blooming
on a bulrush tail

And you wiggled
your scales gleamed
the river lit the moon

Your moon eyes
beheld your mother's shadow
sketching ripples

I unearthed our home
by her dampened grave,
our verge by oceans

There, gray alluvial body
molded her into your gills
you whispered bubbles.

INTERROGATION IN A NAIL SALON IN CALIFORNIA

[How long have you been here?]

> From the airplane window, she saw dragon's eyes
> floating to sheeny green mangrove feet
> its scales a rainbow mirror
> dancing light on her mother's mud wall
> time found its way onto the skin of roofs
> she wondered if home remembered
> or how it sheltered on the
> crumbling field.

[I don't know your place. What does it look like?]

> Her mother's hair: the white river
> her eyes: the blurred pearls blinking
> on heart-lace, carving plumy red
> waggling American flags
>
> Mekong indulged infant cries, feeding
> bitter gourds, more bitter than hardened nails
> Children grew into duckweeds,
> Swaying themselves in sinking joys
>
> The sky was close from Forbidden Mountain
> The Goddess sowed brown-eyed seeds
> Ancient tamarind tree cuddled the clouds
> little humans played hide-and-seek

A child closes her eyes inside a mud mouth.

[Do you want to marry someone and get a Green Card?]

Her tiny nipples
wiped out
a flood of silence

Wedding grew thorns on
woven green coconut gate
burning purple on periwinkle blooms

Her body flinched
by McDonald's yellow sign
cloudy face powder, acetone, nail polish

Phở broth boiled down particles of her night

[I know a man, good person, you can marry him.]

She saw herself in a mirror in a
restaurant toilet at midnight in the
chlorine cloud hallucinating her cracked
fingers. She hid her hands in the janitor's
uniform pocket so that no man could see
how her face was fading into the storm
of keratin dust — spinning manicure
drill.

[Don't worry, nobody knows about your past here.]

Answer: Do you know a service to
change bones?

III

Her past was carved in bones
singing through flood season
Baby herons weep on The Plain of Reeds
Mourning their drowned mother.

[Do you send a lot of money home?]

Her mother sighed.

[Why?]

A slave of borders taped shards of memory
Into a shape of home.

LEGACY OF ILLITERACY

In the school of unraveling words, I wipe the blackboard. My teacher grins and grinds white chalk on the stretch marks of my autopsy. The chalk makes its way from my abdomen to the inner thigh, pressed on the sallow skin, not lively enough to bounce back. My teacher cannot find my vein to inject her unsolicited pity in the shape of vocabulary and math lessons. I am her forensic evidence, intoxicated in her mercy until my breath turns solid in chalk scars.

My neighbor friend chirps by my ears, holding my hand and dipping both of us in the river's stomach until our noses dive under the gray mud, the sky as orange as tear beads carved in our irises. My friend can't hold me long before the teacher goes back to her experiment, shredding me into threads of sacrifice feast, offering my forensic body for any men passing by claiming their protection for our land. An old man with pale palms. Blond men with rotten tongues. Young guys with screeching teeth. I lay in her hand like a stray dog waiting in the front of the school of mercy. No master ever arrives because the monsoon sweeps everyone in floods.

Although it is too late for any remains to trace their paths back to the riverbed, I am patient enough to wait until my teacher gives up on me and throws me into the canal by her Ignorance School, so that I can swim the way back to my neighbor, as if she were still there, diving with a bronze featherback, weaving mangroves into tiny dams, waiting for sweaty breezes to blow my body home.

GRANDPA'S GRAVE

I couldn't find Grandpa's grave after a deep-water season. Water filled a mirror, bemused like a candid child. Grandpa said fishermen grew by water, died of water, and turned into water. I disbelieved as people erected a dike to stop the flow and get abundant harvest. Forever, as they affirmed. At night, Grandpa complained he couldn't die if there was no water coming by. Nowhere to dissolve. A colorful singer danced to her foreign language song on the blinking TV screen. Grandpa said he didn't see human shade for months in the lushy purple forest thirty years before this dike business swept through our lowland. Grandpa's back hurt and he missed the toads' tales from the border town afar beyond purple swarms. I told Grandpa not to confuse layers of life and went back to the pinky K-Pop singer with a twitching dance on TV. That night Grandpa dissolved into water. Dad built a grave on the path to the sea, with sundari mangroves in thickets. Years before all of this, the crocodile was busy enticing passersby for lavish lunch. Grandpa wandered to catch snails and clams searching for honeybees and bulbuls, in the forest turning to fairy tales since the day I was born. In a whim of daydream, my mind couldn't recall where Grandpa's grave was. He watched us beyond the horizon, Dad pointed to the rising tide.

NOTES AND PREVIOUS PUBLICATION

The series of poems about the Hòa Hảo religion are dedicated to the beautiful poetry teaching of Đức Thầy in Vietnamese.

Many poems were constructed based on my years of sifting through The Vietnam Center and Sam Johnson Vietnam Archive of Texas Tech University.

"Karaoke Night in Cần Thơ" found its path through the poem "Karaoke People" by Ed-Bok Lee.

Some of the poems in this project have been honored to appear in magazines, publications, and exhibitions, in various formats and narratives:

- "Interrogation in a Nail Salon in California," winner of the 2022 Academy of American Poets University & College Poetry Prize, *POETRY* magazine (2022).

- "Fish-ing" & "Legacy of Illiteracy," *sin cesar* 12 (2022).

- "The Island Decides to Disappear," *Orion* magazine (2022).

- "Foreign Husbands" and "'Where Girls Are Cheaper Than Air Conditioners,'" *Cha Asian* magazine (2021).

- "Sinking Town," winner of the 2021 Academy of American Poets University & College Poetry Prize, Poets.org (2021).

- "Grandpa's Grave," *diaCRITICS* (2022).

- "Moon Season," the Big Read of Miami Book Fair.

- "The Island Decides to Disappear" and parts of the essay "Erosion" were used as narrative for the Photo and VR exhibition *Shifting Sand* by Sim Chi Yin in the Gropius Bau (Berlin, 2023).

WORKS CITED

Guillemot, François. "Autopsy of a Massacre on a Political Purge in the Early Days of the Indochina War (Nam Bo 1947)." *European Journal of East Asian Studies* 9, no. 2 (2010): 225–65, http://www.jstor.org/stable/23615372, accessed April 11, 2022.

Haseman, John B. "The Hoa Hao: A Half-Century of Conflict." *Asian Affairs* 3, no. 6 (1976): 373–83, http://www.jstor.org/stable/30171434, accessed April 17 2022.

Li, Yiyun. *Dear Friend, from My Life I Write to You in Your Life.* New York: Random House, 2017 (eBook).

Photograph, VA062685. Vietnam Center and Sam Johnson Vietnam Archive, January 23, 1966, Thomas W. Daniels Collection, Vietnam Center and Sam Johnson Vietnam Archive, Texas Tech University, https://www.vietnam.ttu.edu/virtualarchive/items.php?item=VA062685, accessed April 11, 2022.

Sổ, Huỳnh Phú. *Awakening Verses – Book 4.* Harmony Buddhism, https://www.harmonybuddhism.org/448356078?i=179405311, accessed April 17, 2022.

———. *Oracles – Vol. 1.* Harmony Buddhism, https://www.harmonybuddhism.org/450036853?i=179218094, accessed April 17, 2022.

———. *Poem Collection 2.* Harmony Buddhism, https://www.harmonybuddhism.org/445853480, accessed April 17, 2022.